D1404346

Tom Mullen —
Thank you

UNDER ONE
Flag

NEVER FORGET
9-11-2001

Rich Randell

UNDER ONE

Flag

A JOURNEY FROM 9/11 TO THE HEARTLAND

AMY GEORGE RUSH, TOM ROLLINS, AND RICK RANDALL

REEDY PRESS

St. Louis, Missouri

Reedy Press
PO Box 5131
St. Louis, MO 63139
www.reedypress.com

Design by Jill Halpin

Library of Congress Control Number: 2014946019

ISBN: 978-1-935806-54-7

Printed in the United States of America
14 15 16 17 18   5 4 3 2 1

CONTENTS

UNDER ONE

INTRODUCTION

This story charts the journey of one flag pulled from among 2,996 flags displayed in St. Louis, Missouri, to mark the tenth anniversary of the 9/11 terror attacks. That one flag was dedicated to New York City firefighter Michael Weinberg, who died at Ground Zero on 9/11. In a twist of fate, Michael's flag made it into the hands of Larry Eckhardt, known throughout the Midwest as "The Flag Man." As part of Larry's vast collection, Michael's flag flew in Preston, Iowa, along the funeral route of Marine Corporal Zach Reiff, who died while serving his country in Afghanistan. It now rests in Zach's parents' home—a reminder of the tragedy of 9/11 and the wars waged since, and also a symbol for how America's heartland venerates our nation's heroes.

"A NATION REVEALS ITSELF
NOT ONLY BY THE MEN IT PRODUCES
BUT ALSO BY THE MEN IT HONORS,
THE MEN IT REMEMBERS."

JOHN F. KENNEDY

PROLOGUE

An American flag snaps to attention in a brisk November wind that whips across an Iowa cornfield. A man's weathered hands, creases filled with dirt, clutch the flag's metal pole, which is icy to the touch. The man tightens his grip as he drives the ten-foot pole into its designated spot. Posted along a gravel road, the flag flies among thousands of others but has arrived after a singular journey. Remarkable acts of heroism mark the beginning and the end, with acts of compassion forming a connection at the middle. Two men who made the ultimate sacrifice for their country are joined by two men intent on paying tribute. Under one flag, stories intertwine.

 Michael Weinberg 34 New York Fire Department New York NY

INSPIRED

MICHAEL WEINBERG

*I*t's hard to say what golf course thirty-four-year-old Michael Weinberg imagined playing when he practiced putting in his apartment—its threadbare carpet dotted with empty Campbell's soup cans overturned to make perfect targets. As a man who respected the game and played it well, he probably visualized exclusive, exotic courses all over the world. With each clink of a ball on aluminum, did he see ocean in the distance? Mountains? Desert?

On the morning of September 11, 2001, Michael arrived to play a round at Forest Park Golf Course in Queens, New York, a public course nestled in the modest, working-class area where he was born and raised and still lived. Queens is a manageable commute from Manhattan; on a clear day, the tips of Upper East Side skyscrapers are visible from the first tee. Michael hadn't even completed a practice swing when he heard the news that the World Trade Center's Twin Towers in Midtown were burning.

Michael, a New York City firefighter on vacation that day, dropped his golf bag, screeched out of the course's parking lot, and sped to the towers, abandoning his well-worn Ford Taurus on the side of the Long Island Expressway to hitch a ride into the city with an ambulance. He left his cell phone in the passenger seat. With golf now the furthest thing from his mind, he must have been thinking about his older sister Trish Wangerman, who worked on the seventy-second floor

of the South Tower. It's easy to imagine that he would have tried calling her on his way into Midtown.

Michael suited up at his firehouse—Engine 1, Ladder 24—and rushed to the World Trade Center to save lives, including the life of his sister Trish. Ladder 24 captain Daniel Brethel and the Reverend Mychal Judge, fire department chaplain, were with Michael on the ten-block drive to the towers. Upon arrival at the scene, Captain Brethel is widely quoted as telling those assembled, "Guys, be very careful, because firemen are going to die today."

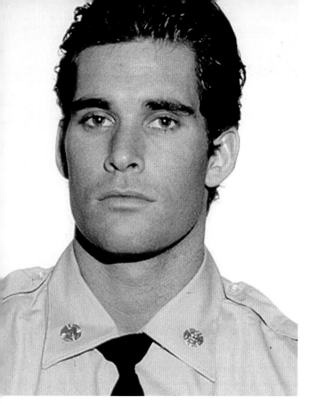

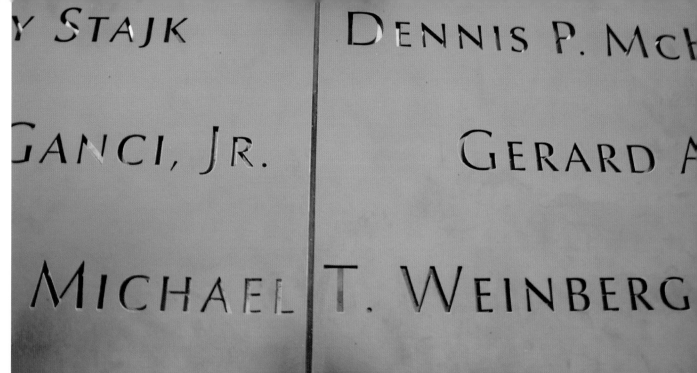

All three men died at Ground Zero. Reverend Judge was killed in the North Tower, from debris of the South Tower's collapse. Michael was killed in the collapse of the North Tower. He was found alongside Captain Brethel underneath a crushed fire truck. Underneath his bunker gear, Michael was wearing his golf shorts and shirt.

Standing on the Brooklyn Bridge when the North Tower collapsed, having no idea of Michael's whereabouts or fate, Trish survived, and now lives in a world haunted by that day's horrors, which she recalls with exacting, nightmarish clarity.

Feeling her tower sway from the impact of United Airlines Flight 175; making eye contact with jumpers through her office window; trusting a gut instinct to leave the building when guards were telling her to lie down, to stay put, to not move under any circumstance; fleeing down a stairwell while passing firefighters were marching up. But no matter what part of her story she chooses to tell, Trish always returns to Michael.

"The people at the golf course said he screeched out of there, just tore out in a blur," she said. "There is no question in my mind that he would have rushed to the towers. But the screeching, that was for me. I know it. I can say that for a fact."

Michael was one of the first victims recovered from Ground Zero. "The man who found my brother told me, 'As I picked him up and put him on a gurney, the first thing I thought: this is a sin; this guy is beautiful,'" Trish recalls. "I never did get to see him. My brother John told the funeral director, 'Make sure that thing, that casket, is nailed shut,' because my family knew I'd try to get in it to be with Michael. And sure enough, as soon as I walked into that funeral home, I went up to the coffin and tried to open it. I stood there and yanked so hard at the handles. That was my baby brother."

Like the man who recovered Michael's body, people were struck by his good looks. He made money thanks to his appearance; as a child, he starred in several television commercials, and he modeled as an adult. Women approached him on the street, handing him their phone numbers—unsolicited. He'd turn to friends and blush, "What am I supposed to do with this?"

Michael was a star athlete as well. He played baseball for four years at St. John's University in Queens, where he was named Most Valuable Player of the Big East Tournament in 1988. After graduation, he was drafted by the Detroit Tigers, but

an injury ended his baseball career. "When he couldn't play baseball anymore, he picked up golf, and he was excellent. Everything he touched he was good at. There's no doubt in my mind that he would have toured one day," said Joe Russo, his baseball coach at St. John's University. "He was that good at golf."

Despite his Greek god–like appearance and athletic prowess, Michael was humble, kind, soft-spoken. He led a modest life replacing one broken down Ford Taurus with another. He was a reliable coworker who clocked in and worked hard, and quietly, on the job. "There's the loudmouth. There's the clown. There's the guy that's always busting chops," said Russ Bakuna, a New York City firefighter who worked with Michael until his death. "He wasn't those guys. He was quiet. He came in; he did his work. He was just a nice guy. He was just a normal guy."

Normal, maybe. A hero, indeed. Everyone who knew Michael expected nothing less than his single-minded mission on 9/11. "When I heard the towers had been hit, the first thing I thought: 'Michael,'" Joe recalled through tears. Of course Michael dropped what he was doing. Of course he fled to the scene on a vacation day and rushed into harm's way while others rushed out. Of course he tried to save his sister and thousands of other innocent victims.

Michael's heroism, and the heroic acts of so many others on 9/11, inspired Americans nationwide. While terrorist attacks tested our nation, the flag that represents our country's fortitude and resilience would continue to fly, atop piles of rubble, at funerals, and half-staff over all our cities. Ten years later, a memorial organized in the Midwest would display flags to honor the thousands who died that day. A flag would fly in tribute to each victim, Michael Weinberg included.

INSPIRED | MICHAEL WEINBERG

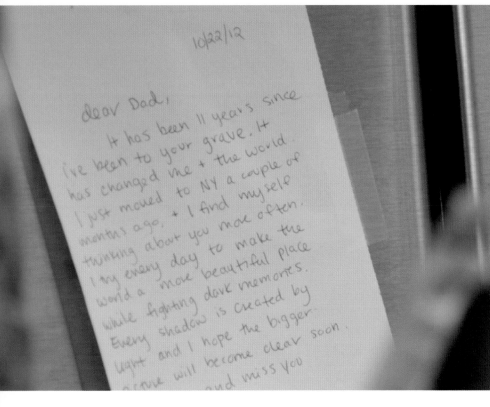

10/22/12

dear Dad,
    It has been 11 years since
i've been to your grave. It
has changed me + the world.
I just moved to NY a couple of
months ago, + I find myself
thinking about you more often.
I try every day to make the
world a more beautiful place
while fighting dark memories.
Every shadow is created by
light and I hope the bigger
picture will become clear soon.
                    and miss you

RHONDA SUE RASMUSSEN   DONALD D. SIMMONS

DIANA B. PADRO   EDWARD V. ROWENHORST   ANGELENE

A L. LIGHTBOURN-ALLEN   CECELIA E. RICHARD

DEDICATED

RICK RANDALL

Rick Randall Jr. lives in Kirkwood, Missouri, a modest, mostly middle-class suburb of St. Louis. It is a throwback, a utopia of sorts for those who appreciate a life uncomplicated by rumbling interstates, un-navigable traffic jams, and towering high rises. Rick and his wife, Susie, live two blocks from "downtown," a vintage train station, a farmer's market, and a snow-cone shack. It's an idyllic life, and Rick knows it. He readily admits, "I'm just a normal guy leading a really great life."

Rick's life, like countless lives throughout the heartland, was rocked by the events of 9/11. While Americans woke to the seemingly same autumn morning, we also collectively experienced the horror of the terror attacks unfolding. As far away as Kirkwood, we could smell the smoke and feel the fear. We too were weeping and grieving, shocked and saddened. We too were moved beyond words and some of us into action, even ten years later.

"9/11 deeply affected me. I never served my country, and I've had guilt about that. And as awful as the terror attacks were, I've seen amazing things come out of them. The way people came together and helped the victims, the way people cared. I just had to do something to mark the anniversary of the attacks," Rick said. And do something he did. Rick and Susie decided to pay tribute to the

2,996 lives lost on 9/11 by creating a flag display in St. Louis to mark the tenth anniversary of the attacks. They thought Art Hill, named for the art museum that sits atop it, was the perfect location. It's the centerpiece of Forest Park, the largest municipal park in the United States, and also the centerpiece of the city itself. It's a place of first dates, wedding photos, impromptu soccer games, and snow sledding races; it's a place where people from across the region gather for Shakespeare festivals and simple picnics. It's also home to a popular municipal golf course. Like Michael's Forest Park Golf Course in Queens, from certain tees, you can see the tops of Midtown St. Louis's taller buildings.

With the vision of covering Art Hill in flags, Rick and Susie set about creating a personalized flag for each victim in their garage. "Pretty quickly we realized our two-car garage in Kirkwood wasn't going to cut it, not for almost three thousand flags." These weren't postcard-sized flags you might wave at a Fourth of July parade; these were three-by-five-foot flags on ten-foot poles adorned with each victim's photo, name, age, place of death, and occupation. Each flag serves as a very personal tribute to each victim. As the garage started to fill with supplies, Rick and Susie knew they would need help. A lot of help.

Rick works in commercial real estate, and as word of his project traveled across his industry's grapevine, benefactors and volunteers stepped forward with offers of supplies, space, and logistical support. "More than five hundred people helped pull this off; it really did take that many people, working down till the last minute, to make this idea a reality"—a large, sweeping, moving reality that touched countless visitors during its week-long installation.

True to Rick's character, the memorial wasn't promoted or advertised. It just went up, and people caught on. Visitors told friends and family, who in turn told friends and family, "You need to see this." The memorial worked like a magnet. Forest Park became congested with visitors in cars, on foot, on in-line skates, in strollers, in wheelchairs, in red wagons. Donations started pouring in.

At the conclusion of the memorial, attendees were invited to "buy" flags for a donation to the Missouri Friends of Injured Marines, the local chapter of the Semper Fi Fund. The first flags to go were the first responders. "The police, the firefighters . . . those just flew off the hill," Rick said. Flags were bought and sent to friends in cities around the world. Several even ended up in New York City firehouses. All told, 2,900 flags found homes, and donations generated by the memorial and its flag sales totaled more than $100,000. "It blew me away. Still does," Rick says. Rick sold all but one hundred flags. He stashed away that batch for a different purpose.

Years prior, he had learned of the work of Larry Eckhardt. Rick and Larry had crossed paths at the funerals of soldiers killed in action in the wars waged since 9/11. Rick creates photo boards of soldiers for display at their funerals. Larry has put up thousands of flags along the funeral procession routes of soldiers from the Midwest. He's known as "The Flag Man." Both are men on philanthropic missions that they perform quietly, on their own time, with their own money. It naturally follows that they would meet and become friends, their mutual respect for one another's efforts running deep.

"I had seen his flags many times," Rick recalls. "I kept thinking, 'This guy is incredible. How does he do this? I have to pitch in.' Our memorial on Art Hill was about honoring and remembering with flags, and that's what Larry's work is about, too. I knew that we could help him. Turns out we did."

Rick donated his stash of one hundred personalized flags from the memorial to Larry, who incorporated them into his growing collection. But Rick wanted to double Larry's collection to total two thousand flags, maxing out the weight limits of his trailer. So Rick gathered the memorial's original volunteers. "We got everyone back together, which wasn't hard. They jumped at the chance to keep things going." The volunteers created nine hundred additional flags for Larry to use at funerals.

Rick delivered the batch of one thousand flags to Larry in his hometown of Little York, Illinois, population three hundred. With Rick's flags added to his collection, Larry would own six flags for every person in his town.

Larry first installed his collection of two thousand flags for the funeral of an Iowa marine killed in Afghanistan during his second tour of duty. Rick made the journey to Preston, Iowa, to witness the impact that thousands of flags make not only on the family and loved ones of the deceased but also on the entire hometown—an impact that Larry has devoted his whole life to making.

NEVER FORGET

41

43

48

COMMITTED

LARRY ECKHARDT

*L*ike Rick, Larry Eckhardt is of the heartland. He blends into the fabric of the region: along with weathered jeans and a logoed jacket, Larry's standard outfit includes stubble and a baseball cap. He stands 5 feet 10 inches when he's not slouching, hands buried in pockets. He's an unassuming man with an equally unassuming lifestyle.

He calls home a makeshift apartment in the basement of a vacant elementary school. A sofa, recliner, and a television set are enough. His hometown of Little York, Illinois, has one restaurant: T&D Sweetwater Grill. Abandoned storefronts beg questions of the past. What used to be? What happened here? Where is everyone?

In 2006, Larry found himself wondering the same. At service members' funerals, he noticed that patriotic displays were lacking or even missing. "There were a few American flags displayed, but in my mind not enough." Larry wondered, where are the memorials? The tributes? The honors? "Where are all the flags," Larry asked himself.

Larry set about answering his own questions. He became committed to shining a light on the war dead by lining their final journeys with the quintessential symbol of sacrifice, honor, and patriotism: the American flag. In doing so, he became "The Flag Man."

He started with one hundred flags that he purchased himself. As funds allowed, he'd add fifty flags here and there. In September 2012, he received the windfall gift of one thousand flags from Rick. Now totaling more than two thousand, his collection often matches the population of the towns he visits. "The trailer can't hold any more. I've maxed its weight limit." The body of his van is packed to the roof as well. "I am the only person in the world who drives a fourteen-passenger van that has only one seat in it," Larry says. The other seats have been removed to make room for flags. Just flags. Between his trailer and van, he transports a show of support unrivaled along the gravel roads and one-way streets that the hearses travel.

Larry has traveled to more than one hundred funerals for service members who've died in the line of duty in the wars waged since the 9/11 terror attacks. "I run my life in four-day increments: travel, set up, funeral, take down," said Larry. "That's all I know." In the hometowns of the war dead, he works on the sidelines. "I am an outsider. The family has more than enough to deal with—what's going on, condolences. Sometimes I run into them later. Mostly I just stay out of the way."

In his 1999 van with attached trailer, he pulls up to a town, usually stopping first at the local VFW hall. From there, word of his efforts spreads organically from mouth to mouth, as he does not advertise or promote his work. Townspeople start to gather with offers to help. These are people who know the deceased. They are family, friends. They are classmates, members of the same church. They are sometimes complete strangers with no connection. But they rally for the same reasons, for something to do, to make something happen, to act on their feelings. To show their appreciation, affection, and love.

Larry is a magnet. He and his work generate devoted interest and commitment from countless strangers. Conversely, Larry is fueled by their participation. Even his appearance transforms. At the center of a group of volunteers, he looks younger, fresher, bright eyed. He is energized into a flurry of action. Just watching him work is exhausting.

Larry motivates, mobilizes, and makes things happen. Without pretense or delay, he digs in. He hands out flags, dispatching rapt listeners with simple instructions about how to plant and display them properly. Throughout the day, he chats with volunteers as if they were old friends, shaking hands, patting backs, and telling jokes. Larry's sense of humor is perhaps the most surprising thing about him. In the midst of such intense work, both emotionally and physically, you wouldn't expect to hear self-deprecating commentary about his failed marriages or his bad habit of smoking. But the jokes keep coming, some corny, some silly, some downright funny. The ease with which he laughs and makes light of life's foibles must ease his burden. How can one bear to witness loss again and again,

amidst so much mourning and grief? You'd have to laugh. "What else am I going to do, cry?" he says. He has a point.

Over a day or two, Larry and the townspeople create a breathtaking display. Scorching sunshine, bone-chilling rain, or Midwestern blizzard, weather is irrelevant. The work gets done. Along the fallen soldier's funeral route, volunteers plant flag after flag attached to ten-foot poles. They trade off using a steel device Larry crafted himself to dig the perfect hole for each pole. The route that the flags create can stretch for miles, a humbling sight to all who witness it.

As grand as his displays can appear, they are overshadowed by the losses they represent. "No town can afford to have this many flags," he says, referring to the voids created when a local service member dies. And Larry really can't afford to do what he does, either.

He sacrifices all that he has to honor each fallen soldier. "The money is just not there," he says. "But all I need to do is get to a town and then back home. That's all I care about." But gas is expensive. He travels on average forty thousand miles a year, to and from service members' funerals—a cost he absorbs himself or that is sometimes covered by unsolicited donations. He eats a lot of hot dogs, because this is what he prefers, he says, but also because this is what he can afford.

And there is the cost to his health. When preparing for and attending funerals, Larry often doesn't sleep for days. He has suffered five heart attacks and undergone triple bypass surgery during his Flag Man years. So getting "there and back" alive is a small miracle. His doctors have pleaded with him to stop planting flags. But as long as service members are dying in Iraq and Afghanistan, he'll keep going.

The funerals sadden Larry and not necessarily in the ways one might assume. "The thing that makes me really and truly sad is that what I do is considered so unique. There should be a person in every state who does this," he says.

"I will be tickled to death when these flags are used just to welcome home the soldiers." He offers a heavy smile, rubs his stubble and resumes the work of unloading flags from his trailer.

On a wintry day in 2011, Larry unloaded those flags in Preston, Iowa. He was there to mark the final road home for an always-faithful, mission-oriented marine who had served his country on two tours of duty in Afghanistan. In Preston, one man and his two thousand flags would say "thank you" on behalf of the community and the entire country.

COMMITTED | LARRY ECKHARDT

BESTOWED

CORPORAL ZACH REIFF

The early morning sunlight cuts across Iowa in late November, the light snowfall from the night before etching out harvested cornstalks, furrowed dark brown earth, and leafless tree branches. At first, silence was only softly broken by the wind blowing across the corn- and soybean-stubbled fields. Then church bells rang out across the small town of Preston, Iowa, bringing home the tragedy of war to America's heartland.

Marine Corporal Zach Reiff had been killed in action in Afghanistan. In the days that followed, Preston paused to honor him. With heavy hearts, this close community struggled to comfort one another and Zach's grief-stricken family.

Zach graduated from Preston High School in 2007. He worked in farming before joining the marines in November 2008. He trained at the Marine Corps Recruit Depot in San Diego, California, where he took to heart the Marine Corps motto, Semper Fidelis ("always faithful"). Zach quickly adapted to the marines and rapidly earned rank and the respect of officers and fellow marines. On his first tour into Afghanistan in 2010, he served with 3rd Battalion, 7th Marine Regiment, 1st Marine Division–Weapons Platoon.

While leading a mounted patrol on July 10, 2010, he was injured by an improvised explosive device (IED) and suffered a traumatic brain injury, shoulder dis-

location, and hearing loss. He spent the next three months recovering in various hospitals, but by October, he returned to Twentynine Palms Marine Base to begin training for redeployment and reunion with his regiment back in Afghanistan.

Zach not only volunteered for service, but he also fought to return to the marines and to Afghanistan. Despite the serious injuries he sustained on the front lines, he felt that he had not yet completed his mission as a marine.

BESTOWED | CORPORAL ZACH REIFF

He rejoined his unit and was promoted to sergeant—the day before he was mortally wounded. Zach was on a combat patrol in Helmand Province, Afghanistan, when Marine Lance Corporal Joshua "Chachi" Corral stepped on a hidden IED. Chachi was killed and the back blast severely wounded Zach. He was airlifted to a field hospital and then transferred to a military hospital in Germany. The nurse aboard the evacuation plane later wrote, "Zach's courage and battle to stay alive to see his parents in Germany would forever be with me and the members of the airlift team." His parents, Marcia and Matt Reiff, made it to Germany to see

Zach; he died shortly after they arrived. He had made it his final mission to say goodbye to his parents.

Zach was forever on a mission. School administrators and coaches remember how teachers and fellow students trusted and respected Zach. He had to work very hard in high school, yet he readily, effortlessly, emerged as a leader concerned primarily with the welfare and safety of others. He helped to build a high school hangout in an old barn a couple of miles outside of town. He and his friends turned cow stalls into rooms, replete with seasoned furniture, old lamps, second-hand appliances, and "John Deere" artwork. A telling sign of Zach's and

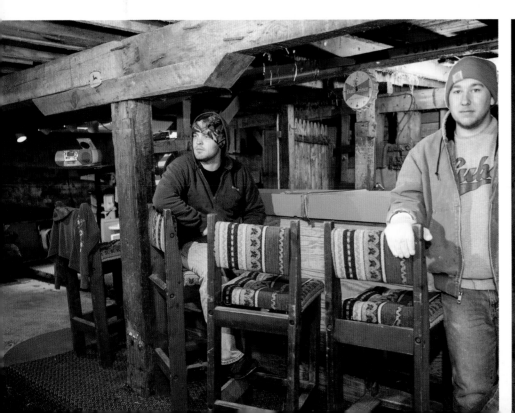

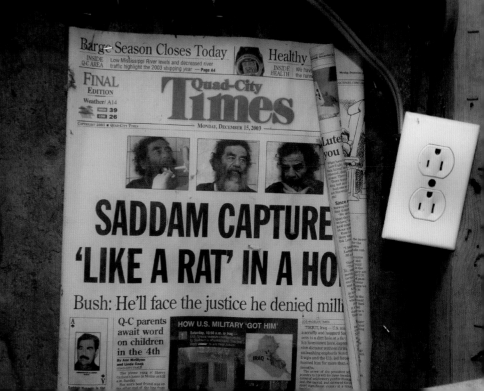

his comrades' patriotism remains on display in the barn: still stapled to a wall, a December 2003 front-page edition of the *Quad City Times* proclaims the capture of Saddam Hussein, "hiding like a rat in a hole." This barn became a safe haven for teenage gatherings. While they had many hours of fun in the barn, they also obeyed a strict policy against alcohol and drugs.

On Zach's last visit home before redeploying to Afghanistan, he returned to Preston High and shared with students his story about the war and his impressions

of Afghanistan and its people. The school is small, with only thirty-four students in his graduating class, and tightly knit. After his visit, students wrote thank-you letters, which were about to be mailed when word reached Preston that Zach had been killed. In response to the tragic news, those same students came together and created artwork honoring Zach. The projects were displayed in other schools and in yards around town as Preston and much of Jackson County, Iowa, prepared to welcome Zach home.

In the front yard of the Reiffs' white, two-story farmhouse, an American flag flies, with the Marine Corps flag below it. At the time of Zach's death, the flags were lowered to half-staff, as were flags across Iowa. The gravel driveway to the house and the dirt road along the barn were packed with pickup trucks and cars. People shuffled from their vehicles and congregated in small groups. Some said nothing, and only their eyes, veiled in tears, told the story of their feelings and suffering. All hesitated before beginning the walk up the hard-packed path leading to the house, first needing to steel themselves to comfort the occupants: parents Marcia and Matt, Zach's sister Emily, brother Kolby, and his wife, Hailey, with Marcia and Matt's grandson Brantley. The visitors' arms were loaded with pans and plates of homemade food, offerings of neighborliness and normalcy to help ease unbearable grief. As they entered the kitchen, the aroma of freshly brewed coffee filled the air as muted conversations, punctuated by weeping and hushed laughter, floated in from adjoining rooms.

Marines who had served with Zach on his first tour in Afghanistan paid him the highest honor. More than a dozen, many now separated from the Marine Corps and striving to establish new lives and careers, traveled from all over America to attend his funeral. They too, one by one, made the difficult walk into the Reiff house to pay their respects in the days before the funeral. Matt reflected, "I know our son was an outstanding marine. Everyone who served with him told us of his valor, courage, and selflessness. The fact so many marines traveled to this funeral from all over the country to be with us and Zach is gratifying and comforting. He will forever be with us."

Zach's personal service awards included a Purple Heart with gold star device, a Combat Action Ribbon, a National Defense Service Medal, a Good Conduct, a Global War on Terrorism Medal, a Sea Service Deployment Ribbon, and the Bronze Star Device.

Zach's funeral was the seventieth funeral that Larry Eckhardt attended with his flag display and the first that would feature his increased collection of two thousand flags. Rick Randall met Larry in Preston for the event. Rick provided a

memorial board of photos of Zach that was displayed in the chapel, and he wanted to see just what two thousand flags looked like along Iowa's farmland roads.

Immediately upon his arrival, Larry went to work, telling all who would listen that "thanks is not enough for young Zach, but it's all we have to give, and we can say it with these flags. Will you help me put them up?" Word spread rapidly. Preston was galvanized into action as hundreds gathered to set about learning to operate sledgehammers and drillers. The frozen ground proved a challenge, but it was obvious from the start that this was for Zach and it had to be done.

Farmers made the fastest progress, accustomed to installing and repairing fence lines. Veterans and legion members worked while telling children, huddled against their parents to avoid the day's chill, the stories and meanings of the American flag. Shopkeepers and tradesmen, Patriot Guardsmen and teenagers, townsmen and country folk pounded the frozen ground and carried poles and flags into the sunset. When they were done, two thousand flags, whipping loudly in the bitter wind, lined the road from St. Joseph's Catholic Church to the small cemetery just outside of town for Zach's final journey.

Gunnery Sergeant Kurtz, the Casualty NCOIC, and a detail of marines had the responsibility of conducting the military funeral. Their task began days before, comforting the family and outlining what would transpire over the next few days. A private jet brought Zach back to Clinton Municipal Airport the day before the funeral. On the tarmac, the marines took possession of his body and remained with him until his burial. Emotion gripped the marine pallbearers. A procession, led by the Patriot Guard Riders, made the twenty-mile journey across the Iowa farmland back to Preston.

Zach lay in state at St. Joseph's Catholic Church for the remainder of the day. The marine detachment provided an honor guard, at his side around the clock.

They stood at parade rest for two-hour watches, and then changed guards with the same precision as if at the Tomb of the Unknown Soldier. After all visitations were concluded, several former members of his platoon returned to spend the last night in the church with Zach.

The following morning a large crowd gathered at the church, and it was very clear it could not begin to handle the number of mourners and visitors for the funeral service, so crowds lined parking lots and sidewalks. Pastor Gregory Geier of St. John's Lutheran Church conducted the service. He said, "I do not believe Zach was a hero because of how he died. I believe he was a hero because of how he lived. Zach knew what it meant to be faithful."

A half-mile-long procession, lined with Larry's flags, departed the church for the cemetery. With Iowa State Police vehicles in the lead, fire trucks and police cars from all nearby communities followed. Patriot Guard Riders preceded the hearse, and the marine detachment and family followed. Citizens lined the route, and the flags, beating in the wind, provided a constant drumming.

The graveside service was brief and simple. The marine guard ceremoniously folded the American flag that had draped the coffin and presented it to the family

on behalf of a grateful nation. Taps played out over the Iowa hills and brought a conclusion to the service. Zach was laid to rest.

After the funeral, Rick walked the way of the flags, admiring Larry's work and thinking about its meaning. He noticed a personalized flag, one of the one hundred "Art Hill flags" that had made it into the batch of one thousand flags he donated to Larry in Little York. Rick was struck first by the photo. The victim

was so young and so handsome. He was struck next by the nature of the victim's work: he was a firefighter who died at the World Trade Center. "How the heck did this firefighter's flag make it to Preston, Iowa," Rick wondered to himself. After all, the first responders' flags were the first purchased, as they generated top-dollar donation amounts. He plucked the flag from the display, respectfully rolled it up, and stowed it in his car to share with Larry. While placing the flag in his trunk, he made note of the victim's name: Michael Weinberg.

Rick connected the dots:

It all came together on the side of that road in Preston. Michael Weinberg died a hero on 9/11, the day all this started. Zach Reiff died a hero on November 21, 2012, in one of the wars that started the day Michael died. And then there's Larry in between, connecting them—a man giving it all to honor and remember our nation's heroes. He wants nothing and gives everything. Just like Michael did, just like Zach did. The three men never knew each other, never will. They looked different, lived different lives, came from different means. But that's not what matters. None of that matters. What matters is that they are three everyday men with extraordinary hearts and passions, who act on their hearts and their passion truly and totally in the interest of others. They are heroes, no doubt about it.

Rick gave Michael's flag to Larry, who presented it to Zach's family as a symbol of gratitude. Under this flag, Zach and Michael were united across a country, over a decade, and through the lives and deaths of thousands who have served in the name of our country since 9/11.

Under one flag our heroes serve, they die, and they are honored. Under one flag our heroes will always be remembered. They will never be forgotten.

94

95

One Year Later

*T*his time the streets of Preston were not lined with furrowing American flags. This time school children did not stand quietly and attentively on curbsides. Red, white, and blue bunting did not festoon the trees, and there were no groups of farmers, townspeople, and patriot riders gathered in hushed clusters along the streets. But this time, like the last, marines were there.

The Reiff family, Marcia and Matt, had now come to know well each of the marines who had served with Zach and who had returned to mark the first anniversary of Zach's death. They came from across the country, not without personal expense, helping each other with rides and pooling money. Gathered on the front porch of the Reiff home, they rejoiced with bear hugs and arm punches, revisited their shared sacrifices, rekindled their camaraderie, and shared stories about Zach. Whiskey bottles and beers were passed around, and cigarettes were bummed with no intention of payback.

For three days the Reiff house and barns rang with the sounds of laughter and memories, country music from Quad Cities station 103.6 filled the farm fields, and hard rock blared from cars in the driveway. For three days the Reiff family prepared huge meals in exchange for their greatest newfound gift, a continued connection to Zach through the men who had stood shoulder to shoulder with him in combat.

On a dark night, sometime between moonset and sunrise, the Reiff family and the marines took the short drive to visit Zach's grave. In that dawn's early light, empty bottles, prismatically reflecting the blackness of a granite headstone, bear witness to their remembrances.

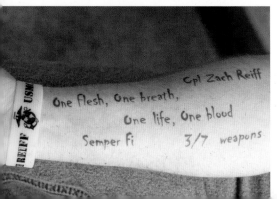

One flesh, One breath,
One life, One blood
Semper Fi   3/7 weapons

Cpl Zach Reiff

100

Epilogue: "Never Forget"

Trish Wangerman

*M*ichael Weinberg's sister Trish fled Ground Zero during the terror attacks, and she didn't go back. "Why would I return? There was nothing left for me there," she said. "My building was gone, I saw massive destruction, and my brother died there. What would be the point?"

In October 2012, Trish found a reason to visit; she saw the point in going back. With firsthand knowledge to share, she wanted to educate her school-age twins about the attacks—all the bad that happened but also the good. So with Alana and Michael in tow, Trish entered the site, now the National 9/11 Memorial, with a mother's focus on reining in her children and meeting their immediate needs. If she had an anxiety or fear, it was well hidden—quelled by the distractions her children provided.

After scurrying through security and filing into the memorial among hundreds of visitors, she found herself standing alone in a gap in the crowd, in a sunny spot on the memorial's grounds. During this brief moment of isolation, she was amazed at what she saw. She kept looking up, but the towers weren't there. So she started looking around.

"This is beautiful. I could cry because it is so beautiful. That's why I could cry, for beauty," said Trish. She went on to explain, "It did not look like this when I left. When I left, it was a war zone. I saw bodies, rubble, papers everywhere, smoke, and thick dust. Now it is peaceful and full of life, too. It is beautiful."

Trish's son Michael, named in honor of his uncle, wore a replica of his uncle's helmet; the original belongs to the National 9/11 Museum. As he rubbed his uncle's

name on the engraved panels that list the names of all the 9/11 victims, onlookers including his sister Alana watched, clearly wondering about the children's connection to the victim. They took photos of Michael and asked him questions. When they learned about his uncle, some started crying. Perfect strangers. The memorial is that kind of place: visitors bring a range of experiences, curiosities, and emotions.

In visiting the memorial for the first time and with her brother's namesake, one would think Trish was ending a chapter, laying to rest painful memories and anxieties. But the visit proved to be a beginning, a watershed moment of possibility. It was the start of talking in more detail with her children about exactly what happened to their uncle, and it was the first of many visits, Trish promised.

"It is a gift to be here. I am proud of this. I will be back again and again," she said.

The journey that Trish took, the memorial that Rick created, and the displays that Larry creates week after week attest to the power of individual Americans to honor and remember the heroes among us—first responders, military, and everyday men and women alike. We honor and remember because it matters. It matters that we thank those who serve our country and our communities, and it matters to visit the places where tragedy took place but also where heroism arose from tragedy's ashes.

For Americans, the flag symbolizes what is good about our country and culture. When we fly the flag, we share its meaning. Whether under 2,996 flags on a St. Louis hill, under more than 2,000 along a rural road, or under just one that unites our heroes, we pay tribute. We honor and remember.

CREDITS AND DONORS

CREDITS AND THANKS

Trish, Alana, and Michael Wangerman

Morty Weinberg

Matt and Marcia Reiff and family

The town of Preston, Iowa

Larry Eckhardt

The town of Little York, Illinois

FDNY Engine 1, Ladder 24

Russ Bakuna

FDNY Lt. James Lane

FDNY Family Assistance Unit

Heidi Drexler Photography

Joe Russo

Jack Kaiser

St. John's University

National September 11 Memorial & Museum

The WTC Tribute Center

Donors

Pace Properties

Guarantee Electrical

Castle Contracting

Mid-America Chevrolet Dealers

Edward Jones

Stock & Associates Consulting Engineers, Inc.

Aon Corporation

Tim Danis and Tom Danis

Jager Creative

ABOUT THE AUTHORS

About the Authors

Every person has his or her unique 9/11 story to tell, as do the creators of this book. On the tenth anniversary of 9/11, their stories converged serendipitously—and a new story was born: *Under One Flag.*

On September 11, 2011, Rick Randall was on St. Louis's Art Hill managing the flag installation he created to mark the anniversary when he noticed a familiar face among the thousands of visitors—Tom Rollins. Tom and Rick had become acquainted through the real estate industry and developed a friendship thanks to a shared love of photography. Tom, a professional photographer, visited the memorial in remembrance—he had lost friends on 9/11—but also to capture through photography the sweeping scene and people upon Art Hill. Rick and Tom talked that day and several times over the course of the memorial's week on display. At its conclusion, Tom shared his images with Rick, who was blown away. Rick knew then that the story of the memorial would live on. But how? In what form?

Also on September 11, 2011, Amy George Rush visited the memorial, recalling the day ten years prior that would change her perspective on life forever. She weaved through rows of flags hand in hand with her husband and young boys, then four and two, reflecting on the lives lost and the hope for a better future. As a professional writer, she naturally channeled her thoughts into a personal essay. She emailed the essay to Rick, with a note of thanks for his work. Rick was moved by her words and knew immediately that he had found the writer of the memorial's story.

When Rick, Tom, and Amy gathered as a team for the first time, their mission seemed simple: document the Art Hill memorial in book form. But then they learned the stories behind some of the flags that had flown on the hill—where they had traveled, what they had meant, and how they connected seemingly disparate people, places, and time periods. They realized their task was much larger than chronicling a week-long installation; the memorial was continuing to serve a far more meaningful, powerful purpose. And once Rick noticed one of the memorial's flags flying on the side of a gravel road in rural Iowa, he knew finally the reason of the team members' coming together.

RICK RANDALL

Rick is senior vice president of development for Pace Properties and the man behind "America's Heartland Remembers 9/11," the memorial that covered Art Hill in St. Louis to mark the tenth anniversary of the terror attacks.

TOM ROLLINS

Tom is a commercial freelance photographer who has worked on assignments on all seven continents. His work has received national awards, is published in books and periodicals, and is collected as fine art. He is a marine veteran of the Vietnam War.

AMY GEORGE RUSH

Amy is an independent journalist based in St. Louis. She has significant experience in public relations, marketing, training, and development. In addition to managing projects and writing, she is editor of a local magazine and an international newsletter.